THE
HARDWARE

THE HARDWARE

Leadership Tools and Tales

Michael Cloutier and
Randi Madonik Skurka

IGUANA

Publisher: Cheryl Hawley
Editor: Kathryn Lane
Front cover design: Ruth Dwight, designplayground.ca

ISBN 978-1-77180-752-4 (paperback)
ISBN 978-1-77180-758-6 (hardcover)
ISBN 978-1-77180-751-7 (epub)

This is an original print edition of *The Hardware*.

For all our children and grandchildren

Contents

Preface

I've always been a storyteller at heart — it's in my bones. That love of stories goes way back to when I was just a little kid, sitting at family gatherings and soaking up every tale my uncles, aunts, cousins, and especially my grandparents would spin. Those weren't just stories to me; they were lessons in life, far better than anything you'd find in a textbook.

Over the years, people have been kind enough to suggest I should write down some of my own adventures. "Mike," they'd say, "you've got stories worth telling." I was flattered — truth be told, I've always been entertained by my own misadventures — but I kept putting it off. Writing isn't exactly my natural talent, while procrastination and I … well, we've been on a first-name basis for a long time.

Eventually, I gave myself a good kick in the pants and decided to call in a professional, someone who really knows how to wrangle words. That's when I met Randi, and I couldn't have been luckier. Somehow, I convinced her that this crazy idea of writing a book might just work.

So here we are, sharing this collection of stories, some from my own life, others from wonderful friends who've let me borrow theirs. We've polished them here and there for dramatic effect, the way movies do, but the heart of each story is true. And Randi? She's the one who made the magic happen.

We hope you enjoy them as much as we enjoyed bringing them to life.

Mike Cloutier

Chapter 1

Small Beginnings

View of Tecumseh Road, Tecumseh, Ontario
Source: www.swoda.uwindsor.ca

The role of leadership is to liberate the potential of the human spirit.

— C. William Pollard

Leadership can be broadly defined as the ability of one person to have an influence on the behaviour of others. In every sphere of life and at every time in history, there have been individuals who have impacted others by visualizing new possibilities that led to breakthroughs in the worlds of business, technology, medicine, and the arts for the betterment of society. Unfortunately, leadership does not always succeed in advancing humanity; history is replete with influential people who have used their knowledge and skill to do great and lasting harm. Leadership is also not confined to matters of great scale and sometimes arises in the most unlikely of places.

Julius Gergley was a grade seven student in the early 1970s, a time when students at a particular elementary school were streamed into three levels. Julius was thought to be a "slow learner" and had been assigned to the lowest "remedial" level. The English teacher was brand new and hadn't been given any curriculum or guidelines; she only had a set of textbooks, mostly primary readers. She had been teaching the class for two months before she realized that most of her students could not read. Thinking back to her own primary school days, she recalled being taught to break words into syllables. She then spent several days with lessons on syllables, feeling quite inadequate as her students did not seem to be catching on.

One day, Julius threw his hand up in the air and exclaimed, "I can do it! I can do it!" He believed that he could show the class how to break words into syllables. "If you hold the back of your hand underneath your chin," he explained, "and speak the word out loud, you can count how many times your chin drops."

"Hmmm," the teacher thought out loud. "Let's try it."

The first word was "window." Win-dow. The chin dropped twice; therefore two syllables.

"Let's try a bigger word," the teacher said.

Julius suggested "refrigerator." Re-frig-er-a--tor. Five syllables. Now the whole class was speaking words out loud with their hands under their chins. They were excited.

The teacher ran to the blackboard and wrote,

Julius Gergley's Law of Syllabication
To determine the number of syllables in a word, just place the back of your hand underneath your chin and speak the word out loud. The number of times your chin drops equals the number of syllables in the word.

Julius had an impact that day. He was a leader. His teacher learned that she could expect new concepts and possibilities from any student, regardless of how they had been categorized. Julius's classmates discovered that they, too, could break words into syllables, and a new way of learning to read had been born. Leaders help others to discover new things about themselves and their abilities. Who knows how many kids went home and showed their parents and siblings what they had learned, whom they, in turn, had instructed, and how many others this idea ultimately reached? A small thing at first, maybe, but Julius had surely helped his classroom and community discover new possibilities in reading.

Everyone is capable of leadership, as it is not so much a position as a role that individuals can step into when the opportunity presents itself.

— Tom Potter, business leader

***

When the hive loses its queen — she alone is able to give life to the colony and maintain order — all seems lost. But the bees do not panic. The worker bees choose a female larva, which would normally become an ordinary worker bee, to receive extra royal jelly, a substance produced by healthy bees that is rich in protein, vitamins, and bioactive compounds. The larva fed exclusively with this special food soon begins to develop differently — the ovaries become active, the body grows larger and stronger, and its lifespan is multiplied by almost twenty.

This bee will not work or follow a routine, but command and give life. She is not chosen based on her genes, but is created, a metamorphosis that saves the entire colony. Once the new queen is ready, she takes over the hive, starts to lay eggs, and restores order, and a new cycle of collective life begins. Threatened with extinction, the colony is reborn stronger, more organized, and more balanced.

And thus we are shown that in times of great crisis, despair is not the way forward, but rather clarity is; we need a plan, a direction; we need to make the right choices and pay attention. In the hive, the queen is not born but supported, nurtured, and guided. Likewise, it is not what we start out with that is important, but what we receive, how we are guided, and what decisions we make in difficult times. It is during those times that the strongest leaders are born — not by chance but by crisis, vision, and transformation.[1]

---

1 Edwin Liava'a, "Honey Bees Are a Surprisingly Great Analogy to Becoming an Alpha Engineer," *HackerNoon*, April 28, 2025, https://hackernoon.com/honey-bees-are-a-surprisingly-great-analogy-to-becoming-an-alpha-engineer.

Photo by Shelby Cohron on Unsplash

Chapter 2

A Package Arrives in the Mail

Delray Beach   Source: Lawrence S. Richardson Jr.

"What is it, Janet? Everything ok?"

She usually texted. Notes of jazz saxophone wafted on the warm Delray breeze as I idled at a red light. Pretty hostesses vied for patrons among those strolling past the little bars with patios spilling onto the sidewalk opposite the beach.

"Yes, fine. Just wanted to catch you early enough to stop at Trader Joe's for a bottle of white, a couple of limes, and some tortilla chips on your way home."

It had been so much fun catching up with the guys after a hectic week with the kids and grandkids visiting from home, that I'd completely forgotten our neighbours were arriving for drinks and a barbecue in an hour. I rubbed my aching knee, turned onto Linton and lowered the sun visor. "You're in luck. Just left the club."

"Ah good. And there's a package."

"I thought we agreed to slow down on the Amazon orders!"

"No, a mail package. Addressed to *you*."

"Really?" Now I was intrigued. "Ok, hon. See you soon."

The lot was busy but I snagged a spot near the entrance and hurried gingerly inside among the Lululemon and tennis-wear clad shoppers. I wondered when I could start golfing again — these long lunches at the Beach Club were making me lazy. *Definitely no more pickle ball — landing on my knee was excruciating as well as embarrassing. Better stick to golf, maybe a little biking*, I decided. Keeping up with those grandkids had been a challenge in itself — I was hardly a college boy. After all, it had been … *four decades* since my SCAAT (Safe Concentration and Assessment Test) days. Had it really been that long?

I kicked off my shoes inside the door and plunked the bags onto the kitchen counter. Janet was nowhere to be seen, but had laid out a lovely charcuterie board, various glassware, a small vase of rose cuttings from the garden, some serviettes and bowls for the snacks, and had stowed all the toys, books, and crayons out of sight. I poured some mineral water and spotted the rectangular, brown-paper wrapped packet with a University of Toronto insignia stamped on its label. *Looks legit enough, though I haven't received mail from them in years. Another fundraising project, most likely.*

Entering my office, I reached into the drawer for a letter opener and my eyes fell on framed photographs of my adorable grandson and granddaughter dressed for Halloween. *Sure is quiet without them.* The package contained a brochure about spring convocation and sponsorship opportunities, and a hand-lettered envelope. I unfolded the heavy cream paper and smoothed it out on the desk. It reminded me of the last letter I had received, which was from the lawyers advising of the process to begin the sale of my grandfather's hardware store and property. My cousin was no longer interested in running it and, though I'd briefly entertained the thought of taking it over, I was torn between fierce loyalty and the knowledge that I lacked the experience, capability, and time to do so. But powerful memories had flooded back, making me realize the enormous influence of the Hardware on my life's work — it was the end of an era.

I looked at the letter spread out on my desk.

> February 1, 2025
> Dear Bradley Stuart,
> On behalf of the University of Toronto, I am pleased to inform you that the university's Governing Council has elected to award you an Honorary Doctorate in recognition of your outstanding contributions to business education. This distinguished honour reflects your exceptional achievements, dedication, and the positive impact you have made on both your community and the world at large....

My eyes caught the sepia wedding portrait on my desk — my young parents, slim and elegant in their modest finery, their faces hopeful. I misted up a bit imagining them looking down on me with unabashed pride. It sent a shiver down my spine, but it was a warm, comforting shiver. Beyond the portrait, the wall was lined with books collected over a lifetime — on business leadership, world religions, philosophy, and politics. These tomes had shaped my thinking with lessons gleaned, practised, and passed on to children and students, with *Good to Great: Why Some Companies Make the Leap ... and Others Don't* by Jim Collins the most prominent.

> Your work has exemplified the values of excellence, innovation, and service that are central to the mission of the University of Toronto. It is with great admiration that we celebrate your remarkable career and the lasting legacy you have created in your field....

"What's new at the university?" Janet walked in wearing a gauzy white blouse, fastening a silver earring, her dark hair pulled back, bronzed skin glowing. *I am one lucky bastard*, I thought. She frowned as she picked up the box of Kleenex from the sideboard and placed it on the desk. I blew my nose and handed her the letter, and as she began to read aloud, her face broke into a wide grin and she looked at me, dark eyes twinkling.

"With my luck, it's just another scam," I said.

"Don't be silly!"

> We would be delighted if you could join us at our upcoming ceremony, scheduled for June 15 at Convocation Hall, and honour us by addressing the graduating class of MBA students with a keynote speech.

"What wonderful news! All the more reason to raise a glass — I'll pop open the prosecco." She wrapped her arms around my shoulders and kissed my cheek. "Why don't you go change?"

I threw on a black linen shirt and jeans, combed my hair, and put my favourite playlist on speaker, then joined Janet by the pool for a preliminary glass of bubbly. She called up the kids and grandkids on her tablet for a quick FaceTime session to share the news. As my mind wandered back to Tecumseh and the Hardware, I thought about calling my sister and her family, too. *Tomorrow will work just as well,* I decided.

Chapter 3

The Hardware: Memories of Tecumseh, Windsor, and Motor City

Robinet Grocery and Meat Market, Tecumseh, Ontario
Source: www.swoda.uwindsor.ca

Tecumseh, Ontario, was the place of my birth — well, technically I was born in a Windsor hospital — and that of my parents. Named for the great Shawnee chief, one of the most prominent Indigenous figures in Canadian history,

Tecumseh was a man who strove to unite his people, a bridge builder as well as a fierce warrior.

I returned to Tecumseh every summer of my childhood and stayed with my grandparents, after my family moved to the Greater Toronto Area. My grandfather's family business was a hardware store, and everyone in town knew him. It was in an old, historic building with creaky wooden floors and dust motes floating in the rays that slanted through the window into the dimly lit aisles. I'd help out there once I got older, but as a kid, just hanging with my cousins and friends was like heaven — listening on my tinny transistor radio to Detroit Tigers games in the evenings or to Motown hits on sweltering afternoons under a shady tree.

Some days I'd ride my bike down a dusty gravel road to the schoolyard and join a pickup game of baseball, where we'd take turns at bat and circulate positions in the hot sweet air, the hum of farm trucks and cicadas filling the afternoon. I'd borrow a handle from the hardware store to turn on a spigot so we could gulp some water from the splashing stream. Later, I'd bike to the hardware store — the neighbourhood gathering spot — where I'd fish a few nickels and dimes from my pocket for a bottle of Coke, ice cold from the pop machine. The fizz tickled my nose as I took a sip. The caps would collect at the bottom of the machine, and, courtesy of my grandfather, I'd win quite a few contests that way!

Often, I'd head toward the Detroit River, park my bike and watch ships and boats glide by, wondering where they were headed. As the sun began to sink, it was time to head home before the streetlights flickered on; the smell of Mem's cooking — maybe fresh perch and corn on the cob — would welcome me inside.

Detroit had always fascinated me; it was the Emerald City to our quaint little town. If I was lucky, Mem and Pep would take me over to shop or for lunch. And when Dad visited, we would sometimes take the short bus trip through the tunnel to a game at Tiger Stadium, where he'd treat me to a Ball Park Frank and a Coke. There was no better hotdog in the world than at Tiger Stadium. It never ceased to amaze me that we could travel under the river from one country to another. Standing on the bank of the river in Windsor, Detroit didn't seem very far away, but riding the bus through the tunnel made the minutes seem like hours, especially when I'd be imagining the whole thing collapsing and filling with rushing Great Lakes' water. Inevitably we would emerge and be left blinking in the sunlight when the bus dropped us off a few blocks from the stadium.

I'd look up in awe at the gleaming skyscrapers of Motor City. Occasionally, we would walk through some rough areas, skid rows, where homeless, alcoholic or drug-addicted people would lean in doorways or sit right on the sidewalk and beg for spare change. Dad would give me coins for them, reminding me later to be grateful for the comfortable home and life I shared with my family — food on the table, a roof over our heads, occasional treats, special days like trips to baseball games with Dad. As I got older, I appreciated these blessings more and more; these experiences provided a sense of humility and sensitivity towards others who had much less.

On the other hand, television, radio, and magazines were providing a window into a world of interesting people and exciting places — travel, cars, and upscale lifestyles with fabulous toys, filling me with ambition. I wanted those, too! It was a big world and the good life was out there somewhere for the taking. Though I appreciated my good fortune in a simple upbringing, I wanted to strive for more, for excellence in all that I did.

Once we got to the stadium with its hustle and bustle, sights and smells, we would descend to the ground level.

We'd always arrive early to watch batting practice, and I could barely contain my excitement — bats cracking, so close we could hear the players conversing. Trips to Tiger Stadium with Dad are my fondest memories. Even now, when I watch a game at the new Comerica Park stadium, I can still smell the heady mixture of fresh cut grass, popcorn, and my dad's pipe smoke enveloping me in sheer happiness, contentment, and safety.

But in the summer of 1967, the Detroit race riots shattered my innocence. Their violence — the fires and tragic death toll, the extensive destruction ignited by the police raid of an unlicensed, after-hours bar — was devastating. The catastrophe was captured by Gordon Lightfoot the following year in his song "Black Day in July," which was broadcast in Canada but was banned in thirty American states. Motor City madness had indeed taken over the countryside, while the song's opening phrase itself took on a life of its own.

I asked my grandfather about Tecumseh, Windsor, and Canada's history.

"Is there racism here too, Pep?"

"There certainly is, Brad, I'm sorry to say. There was a time when Black people were in danger if they were seen in town at night. But things have improved, continue to improve. Many towns and places in southwestern Ontario were eventually listed in the *Green Book* of safe havens for Black people to travel to. And don't forget, more than a century ago, Chatham was the northernmost stop on the Underground Railroad, which helped tens of thousands of people reach freedom from slavery in the US. That's where Cubs pitcher Fergie Jenkins was born."

My interest in politics and world affairs had been sparked, but there were no visits to Tiger Stadium for two summers. Today the area is home to burgeoning Indigenous,

Lebanese, and Russian Mennonite populations and growing numbers of Jamaican and Latino restaurants.

After I turned fourteen, I stayed back home to work at summer jobs picking fruit and vegetables, cutting lawns and eventually, at a grocery store. Thus began the process of saving up money so I could put myself through community college, limiting time spent in Tecumseh to infrequent trips to see Mem and Pep. Once I bought my first car, an old beat-up Mustang, I could travel there for the day on my own. I miss that car sometimes. It reminds me of how important the auto industry was to my family back in Windsor, and I wonder — with concern — about the future of an important economic driver and significant employer.

***

What a year 2025 is turning out to be — tariff threats and a Canadian election looming, stock market fluctuations, ongoing wars abroad, I thought, distracted as I prepared the barbecue. For the first time in my life, I was worried about the future of Canada — national security, public safety, economic stability, free trade. My keynote speech would have to be an extra inspiring one to counter the new uncertainty — and the flagging Canadian spirit and dollar. There was one good thing about the turmoil emerging across our borders: we were being forced to think about our identity as a nation. What are our values? Are we going to let others define us, control us? What a tremendous leadership challenge!

I looked out beyond the terrace at the perfectly groomed links, the pretty orchids and palm trees, the herons stepping languidly from the pond onto the green in the golden light of dusk. I hadn't thought twice about being Canadian until recently. I had to admit, there is much I'd taken for granted:

a small-town upbringing, simple hardworking parents and grandparents; old-fashioned values that I'd hopefully passed on to my kids. I'd achieved everything I'd set out to do —even surpassing my own expectations — through opportunity, hard work, and, in all honesty, amazingly good luck. Though I've had a good life, over the last decade I'd become unimpressed, then downright impatient with the way things had become in Canada — the stagnant economy, the sense of less-than-average standards becoming acceptable to far too many people, in my opinion. I had even considered a permanent move south.

But over the last year the ground had shifted, and the freedoms I'd always taken for granted were now under attack. What did it mean to be Canadian? What is unique about us, worth protecting, worth preserving? Canada has always been the mosaic, the wonderful amalgam of diversity, infinitely more valuable as a whole than the sum of its parts; a country of many blessings — a beautiful country of abundance and freedom. But where had our drive for excellence, for success — not just economic, but civic, as members of society — disappeared to?

Sure, it was flattering to be recognized by the university. But I now realized it was time to summarize all the things I'd learned over the decades, to crystallize them, highlight the tools from my experience to help navigate an uncertain future, not just in work, but in life. We need to be resilient, courageous, open-minded, and open-hearted change leaders; we need to strive, always, for excellence in all our endeavours. We must be the best we can be as individuals, family, and team members, in communities and as global citizens.

KEY TAKEAWAYS

- **Character First** Leadership grows from humility, discipline, and early responsibility shaped by family and small-town values.
- **Lead with Empathy** Injustice fuels moral responsibility, inclusiveness, and compassion.
- **Gratitude Grounds Ambition** Balanced leaders value both stability and striving.
- **Think Globally, Stay Rooted** A blend of rural grounding and urban insight creates visionary leadership.
- **Inspire to Elevate** Great leaders use their experiences to serve others with clarity, courage, and purpose.

Chapter 4

The Grapevine: Networking and Communication

Sandwich Street winery building, Windsor, Ontario, c. 1895
Source: www.swoda.uwindsor.ca

The single biggest problem in communication is the illusion that it has taken place.

— George Bernard Shaw, playwright

As I had perused the wine selection in Trader Joe's earlier that day, I was reminded of my great-grandfather Jacques — Pep's father, a legendary winemaker of the Windsor region, and, though I was born long after his death, a huge influence on my life. Landing in Canada with little more than a knack for business picked up from his trader father and a lot of ambition, Jacques arrived in Essex County after the family fled the ravages of the Franco-Prussian War from the region of Burgundy, France. He parlayed his first business as a travelling tinsmith into various enterprises, most notably wine production, as well as a prosperous grocery store in Tecumseh, which eventually became the Hardware. Jacques and his father Georges began by cultivating a vineyard according to their ancestral traditions, which went back five centuries in France. As this business and other enterprises grew and flourished, Jacques provided employment to many family members and fellow immigrants from the same region of France He became a pillar of his community to whom many would turn for shelter, financial support, and legal advice over the decades.

Always the creative thinker, Jacques brought many innovations to his winemaking, experimenting with fermentation of various fruits, trying different varieties of grape, and expanding into the production of cider and sparkling wines. At harvest time, he would sell grapes and grape juice to Quebec wineries, local jam manufacturers, and sacramental wine producers for the Catholic Church, or at fairs and markets on both sides of the border. He also devised a door-to-door delivery service and established a rail depot next to his property to facilitate transport of his products.

Jacques used his way with people and vast network of social contacts to expand his wine business, which survived through Prohibition, and also to assist his family and friends in times of need. He was deeply involved in community service, sitting on the board of the separate school and on town council, and was a devoted member of his church throughout his lifetime. He was a leader in every sense of the word, one who left his mark on his town and its citizens, for the betterment of all, and one that I strive to emulate.

Vineyard, Sandwich, Ontario.
Source: www.swoda.uwindsor.ca

***

Leaders build and maintain relationships, as I learned on those early mornings with my grandfather at the Hardware, watching him and other relatives connect with clients, neighbours, friends, and family. For me, creating strategic relationships with key stakeholders has been vital — from the time I was a sales rep right through my career as an executive leader and CEO — to support business objectives and to advance from one level to the next. But equally valuable are those connections I've made based on finding common elements with almost anyone I meet. I still correspond with school friends, former teammates, and people at all levels in places I have worked through LinkedIn, for example, or by meeting regularly over coffee, a meal, or drinks. Early on, I approached leaders I admired to meet with me, and over time

I began to meet with colleagues and young people to hear their point of view and sometimes to mentor them. I invariably learn a great deal from almost every encounter and conversation I have. Great leaders are also great listeners and lifelong learners, and I have found that the more open you are to others, the more trust and confidence you inspire.

While some leaders compete their way to advancement and see the opportunity to lead as a struggle against others in a zero-sum game, a true leader is one that is lifted up by others, one that never degrades nor demeans those around them, but instead pursues *external* competition — for market share, continuous improvement, sustainability, and people development; one who advances not themself alone, but the mission of the team, the organization as a whole. A true leader never fears that their colleagues may excel beyond them — fear and jealousy are not leadership qualities. A leader provides honest feedback, the kind that helps others improve in their roles.

As a leader, people look to you not just for guidance, but for your example — how you embody authenticity in a role. One area where many leaders struggle is giving feedback. We worry, *Will this hurt someone I care about? Will my words cut too deep?* And if so, does that change what the person receiving the feedback actually hears?

I've been guilty of softening the message. For example, when someone didn't get a job, I might have said, "Hey, you did great. I know you're disappointed, but there's nothing you need to work on — just keep at it, and you'll be in a great position next time." But does that really help them understand why the decision went the other way? Does it give them a clear sense of the gaps they need to close? Not at all.

Early in my career, I was fortunate to have mentors who practiced what I call "honestly helpful feedback." This meant feedback from the head — clear, thoughtful insight into what I was doing well, where I was struggling, and what might hold me back — along with the most important feedback, which was from the heart. There's something powerful about a leader saying, "I have some feedback that might be tough to hear. I'm sharing it because I care about you and want you to succeed. I'll be here to support you. Are you open to hearing it?" I've received feedback that kept me up at night, but it was exactly what I needed to hear. And because I knew the person cared, I could listen to it and act on it. That question, "Are you open to hearing it?" is incredibly powerful. It sets the stage for trust, honesty, and growth. As leaders, we must give and invite honestly helpful feedback. It's a two-way street. And when we model it, we show what authentic leadership truly looks like.

It is important to remember the concept of a leader as coach. John Whitmore, in his book *Coaching for Performance*, does an excellent job in outlining how leaders help others to identify their goals and help them see the gap between where their skills are today and where they want them to be. He delineates how a leader must ask the members of the team to identify what opportunities they can pursue for growth and must also ask for permission when suggesting other avenues. Finally, it is crucial to ask what they are willing to commit to doing for their growth, and how the leader can help with feedback and support.

KEY TAKEAWAYS

- **Legacy of Leadership Through Service** Visionary leadership is rooted in innovation, generosity, and deep community engagement.

- **Relationship-Centered Approach** Effective leaders build and nurture meaningful relationships across all levels — clients, peers, mentors, and mentees — not for self-promotion, but to foster trust, shared growth, and mutual respect.

- **Strategic Networking** Personal and professional advancement is supported by deliberately forming authentic, strategic connections — leaders listen well, seek out diverse voices, and stay connected to their broader ecosystem.

- **Communication as Culture-Building** True leadership involves not just transmitting information, but ensuring understanding, connection, and alignment. Great leaders communicate with openness, humility, and a genuine desire to learn.

- **Lifting Others Up** Leadership is not a zero-sum game. The strongest leaders do not compete against their colleagues but champion their success. They focus competition outward — toward innovation, excellence, and collective progress.

- **Honestly Helpful Feedback** Modelling, sharing, and accepting frank feedback ensures growth.

Chapter 5

Honorary Degrees and

Commencements

Convocation Hall, University of Toronto
Photo by Kara M on Unsplash

I swept the fallen leaves and gathered the debris that the wind had scattered across the patio. It was quiet work, but purposeful. I have always believed that cleanliness, both in our surroundings and in our conduct, is an outward expression of respect for others, and in this I follow Janet's lead to provide not only comfort, but true hospitality to our guests.

***

I remembered my own convocation where the speaker was Maurice Koffman, a man of wealth, but more importantly, a man of conscience. He spoke with earnest sorrow about Indigenous communities in Canada — about the children taken, the lives disrupted, and the deep suffering that had been imposed under the pretence of education and progress. He reminded us that for a hundred years, voices had been silenced, and justice denied. It is a terrible thing when a system is used not to elevate but to erase. But even in such pain, there are seeds of renewal. Maurice had worked with Indigenous leaders and corporate allies to create a path of economic self-determination. He did not simply speak of reconciliation; he acted upon it. I have never forgotten his example.

Many years passed, and I was called to serve as president of PharmaLabs. In that role, I was invited to mentor young minds at the University of Toronto. I accepted not with pride, but with humility. To teach is not to instruct, but to walk beside others, learning always. Later, I was asked to help raise funds for a new student resource centre, to be named after Mayor Gertrude McPhee. "Trudy the Tornado" was known for her courage on the hockey rink and her fierce commitment to justice in public life. Her example was not only in her victories, but in her perseverance.

I recall how nervous I was when I met her. My smile betrayed my awe, and Carrie Fley, my liaison and trusted friend, leaned close and whispered, "She won't bite." It was a small kindness, but one that helped me to break the ice. In the months that followed, Carrie and I became companions in a common cause, and I found in her a spirit of quiet strength and generosity. It has often been the case in my life that those I was meant to guide ended up guiding me.

Trudy, as we fondly called her, joined us for many long lunches. We spoke not only of fundraising but of life, persuasion, and building unity among people with different views. We shared laughter, sherry, and sometimes silence. In these conversations, I saw again the importance of truth spoken with compassion and disagreement carried without hatred. This was exemplified by the dynamic relationship between Trudy and our honorary chair of the new student resource centre, "Halton Harry" Dawson, once premier of Ontario. Though they disagreed often and publicly, their mutual love for the people bound them. That is the essence of democracy — not uniformity, but unity in purpose.

Carrie was the heartbeat of our committee. As we grew closer, we shared burdens and small disappointments. Once, her assistant left unexpectedly during a critical time. I remembered a similar moment in my own career. I told her about a man I had mentored who chose to leave for a rival. I was hurt, but I chose to respond with grace and offered him a letter of recommendation. In truth, our responses to adversity reveal our character more than our triumphs. Carrie listened, and in time, she too made peace with her assistant. On another occasion, I unknowingly served on a board with her mother. We had spoken glowingly of one another's contributions, never knowing the connection. It was a simple moment, but a powerful reminder: sincerity is never wasted.

Carrie's path led her to the Senate of Canada. I would never take any credit for her rise — her own merit carried her — but I feel joy in knowing I played a very small part in her journey. That is the true measure of influence: not domination, but gentle encouragement that helps another to grow.

***

My thoughts were interrupted by laughter on the patio. Janet had welcomed our friends Lisa and Dave, and we were each handed a glass of prosecco.

"To Brad, and his upcoming honorary doctorate!" Janet exclaimed. "So proud of you, honey!"

"Cheers," came the reply.

And I smiled, not because of the honour, but because I was surrounded by love, and by people who had grown with me, as I had grown with them. In such company, there is no need for titles. There is only gratitude, and the quiet joy of sharing and celebrating meaningful moments together.

KEY TAKEAWAYS

- **Respect Begins with Small Acts** Cleanliness, hospitality, and thoughtfulness reflect care for others and attention to character.
- **Lead with Conscience, Not Just Credentials** True influence comes from taking action on values, not just speaking about them.
- **Teach by Walking Beside, Not Above** Mentorship is a shared journey of learning and growth.
- **Grace in Adversity Reveals Character** How we respond to disappointment defines us more than our successes.
- **Real Leadership Is Quiet Influence** The goal is not to control, but to uplift and empower others to thrive.

Chapter 6

Presentation Meltdown:

Support, Loyalty, and Respect

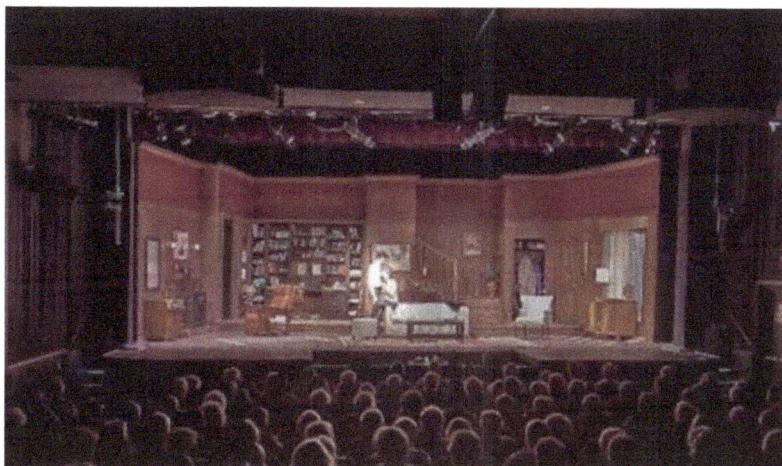

Delray Beach Playhouse.
Source: www.delraybeachplayhouse.com

The next evening we took in a play with friends from further down the coast, arriving last minute and rushing to our seats as the lights dimmed and the conversation quieted in the playhouse auditorium. As the curtain went up and a lone actor stood on the stage, decorated as the ornate dining car of a steam train, I was reminded of a time long ago, early on in my career, when I stood before a roomful of my peers ready to perform.

***

We were at a cycle meeting — a regular gathering of the team held every few months, to discuss field force, or strategies and resources then taken to district sales meetings. These gatherings were always full of vibrant discussion, and there was nothing particularly high pressure about it. I was used to speaking in public. But I had an uneasy feeling standing at the front of the room that day.

Now on the marketing staff and before that in sales, I had always had strong relationships all around. I was even able to develop a close rapport with senior leaders, utilizing a broad range of interests and an insatiable thirst for knowledge. My new boss was very young, as well as extremely bright, dynamic, and capable. We connected over sports, and I'd opened my home to him as he was single and in a new country. Although we were friends, I felt little respect for him as a leader; he seemed to me an up-and-coming marketing star that no one had taken the time to instruct in the finer points of leadership. Feeling isolated and increasingly unsupported as time went on, I began to doubt myself, uncertain of my role or of my future. My confidence was eroded little by little, the tension mounting until it was my turn to make a presentation to the team. There were about twenty people in the room.

I began my presentation, but midway through it, I just froze! I had completely lost track of my train of thought. As the seconds ticked by and I looked out at the faces of my colleagues, their expressions turned from encouraging smiles and looks of interest to those of anxiety and concern. My scattered thoughts and confusion gave way to alarm and panic. After what seemed like an eternity, a sales manager colleague and mentor came to my side at the front of the room and announced that we would all take a quick break. He walked me over to the back and poured us each a glass of water.

"Now Brad," he said quietly, "take a few deep breaths, collect yourself, and let *him* take over. I have your back. *We* have your back."

I took some sips of water and a few deep breaths and instantly felt grounded. After a few minutes, my boss had wrapped up my talk and the meeting continued on without any further issues. Colleagues came up to me afterwards and reassured me that all was well, that I had their support. I realized two important things then. Firstly, that the investment to build a strong network of trust and respect allowed me to continue with peer support. And that the uneasy feeling, my increasing loss of confidence, was trying to tell me something — it was time to move on to another role. Fortunately, the sales department reached out with offers of promotion and I was able to stay in the company. But I never forgot the words of encouragement, the quick action, and the simple sense of caring and concern that I received that day. I have passed on that lesson many times to those I coached and mentored over the years.

***

Another incident came to mind, this one relayed by my colleague Mira who was met with an unexpected challenge by a superior and opted for the high road:

> Towards the end of my career, I worked for a company where the CEO was in his 80s. During a particularly challenging negotiation, I went to his

office to provide an update and highlight some of the sticking points.

After listening, he looked at me and said, "We need to get this deal done. Do what you need to do, but be careful — these people are very smart, talented, and tough. You know what these Indians are like."

I looked at him, somewhat surprised, and replied, "Yes, yes, I know what Indians are like — I'm Indian."

He immediately became flustered, backpedalling. "No, no, I didn't mean you! I don't see you as Indian — that's not what I meant."

I let him carry on talking for a moment or two. At the time, I wasn't sure whether to be offended or flattered or simply chalk it up to generational bias. He was, after all, an elderly man from a different time.

Later, as I reflected, I found myself caught somewhere between being amused and being insulted. But ultimately, I chose to take it in stride and focus on the task at hand.

We concluded the negotiations successfully. When I told him we were ready to sign, he smiled and said, "I knew you could do it. You Indians — you know business. I was sure you'd succeed."

To this day, I'm not quite sure whether that was a compliment, a stereotype, or something in between. But what I took from the experience was this: sometimes, in leadership and in life, we're faced with moments that test our perspective, requiring us to stay calm and carry on with grace — even when your first inclination may be anger or the thought of retaliation.

The lights came up and it was time for intermission. *Bring on the popcorn!* I thought as I rose to leave the auditorium.

KEY TAKEAWAYS

- **Strong Networks Create Safety Nets** Trust and respect within a team can carry you through moments of vulnerability.
- **Pay Attention to Inner Signals** Persistent unease or doubt may be a cue that it's time for change or growth.
- **Leadership Isn't About Titles, It's About Care** One moment of compassion can shape a person's trajectory and mindset for years.
- **Pass the Support Forward** The best leaders pay forward the empathy and mentorship they once received.
- **Navigate Bias with Poise** Generational or cultural bias may surface in leadership contexts; handling it with maturity preserves relationships and influence.
- **Leadership Is Emotional Intelligence in Action** Balancing self-awareness, restraint, and empathy is key to leading through uncomfortable or ambiguous moments.

Chapter 7

Driving Sandy: Authenticity

Photo by Allison Saeng on Unsplash.

Be yourself; everyone else is already taken.

— Oscar Wilde

Early on in my tenure as a newly appointed sales manager — ambitious, hopeful, and a bit green behind the ears, I found myself, one afternoon, behind the wheel of a company car, tasked with a rather unexpected responsibility: ferrying Mr. Sandy Blanderson, the firm's head of US commercial operations, to the airport.

Now, Mr. Blanderson was not merely a man of stature in the organizational hierarchy, but a veritable colossus of corporate charisma. Picture a figure that might have stepped out of an Edward Hopper painting, if Hopper had ever dabbled in depicting *GQ* covers — broad-shouldered, blue-eyed, and blond, with a jaw so square it might have been borrowed from a sculpture of some half-forgotten Roman god of commerce. His handshake — firm, dry, and utterly confident — seemed to bind you in a temporary contract of mutual attention.

I must confess I was more than a little in awe. Terrified, even. But Mr. Blanderson had the good manners and natural showmanship of someone who had long ago discovered that the best way to command a room — or in this case, a vehicle — was not to talk about himself, but to ask questions. And so he did.

"How's business?" he began, effortlessly. "What do you love about your work?"

The queries kept coming and I, perhaps flattered beyond reason, answered each one with an earnestness that surprised even me. There I was, a junior man on the make, suddenly speaking with candour about what made our team tick. I spoke at length — too long, probably — about my colleagues, their strengths and foibles, and how the collective spirit, the esprit de corps, gave our team its edge. I may have even missed the exit ramp. It hardly mattered.

When we reached the airport, he took my hand in his bear grip, thanked me for the ride and the conversation, and strode off towards departures with the confident gait of a man who is always upgraded to first class.

Back at the office, I was called over by my boss, who looked at me with a peculiar grin.

"What happened on that drive?" he asked, as if I'd thrown a martini in Mr. Blanderson's face.

I gulped. Had I overshared? Spoken out of turn? Was I, in fact, about to be demoted for showing excessive enthusiasm?

"Sandy was so impressed with you, he wants you promoted immediately!"

My relief was so overwhelming, it bordered on giddiness. I blurted, "So when is my promotion?"

My boss, now grinning like the Cheshire Cat, replied, "It's not today, son. So get back to work."

And so I did.

***

A few years later, Sandy Blanderson died. I remember hearing the news and being unable to process it at first. He was the sort of man who seemed indestructible; too composed, too alive to be undone by the randomness of fate. I was shaken. It was the first time I'd lost someone I'd admired from up close.

Lessons learned: several, and they've stayed with me.

First: Never underestimate the impact of a genuine conversation. What I took to be small talk was, to him, a litmus test of leadership. And I passed, not by proving my own brilliance, but by illuminating the strengths of others.

Second: Admiration needn't require long acquaintance. We can be shaped by brief encounters, if we are paying attention.

And lastly, perhaps most poignant of all, I learned that even the brightest lights are vulnerable to the dark. That life is not always measured in years or titles, but in presence, in moments. And that any moment may be our last. Which is why, to this day, I try — imperfectly but earnestly — to give each moment its due.

KEY TAKEAWAYS

- **Conversations Reveal Character** Genuine curiosity and thoughtful listening can identify emerging leaders more than credentials can.
- **Celebrate Others, Not Yourself** Highlighting your team's strengths builds trust and signals true leadership potential.
- **Brief Encounters Can Shape Us** Even short interactions can leave lasting leadership lessons — if we're paying attention.
- **Presence Matters More Than Position** Leadership is often felt in moments, not titles.
- **Life Is Unpredictable — Lead with Heart** Every moment counts; approach each one with respect, humility, and intention.

Chapter 8

Personal Heroes: Resilience and Adapting to Change

Photo by Waldo Malan. Source: Unsplash.

The next morning dawned with the grim efficiency of a boarding school headmaster banging on the door of yet another wasted adolescent. Janet, ever the cheerful capitalist, was wearing a skort; she bounded off to the golf course with her well-preserved friends, ladies who bore the calculated ease of those who have survived three husbands, two facelifts, and a handful of fundraisers for obscure diseases. I, meanwhile, stumbled into my trainers and limped towards the gym, dragging along a modest sense of purpose and a slightly swollen knee that had become my constant companion.

I began to go through the regimen my trainer, a man half my age with twice my enthusiasm, had crafted for general fitness and to strengthen my knee. It combined the punishing monotony of cardio with the light humiliation of yoga. There were free weights, too; just enough for some semblance of dwindling masculine prowess. So, like an aging knight preparing for battle, I mounted the elliptical and began to churn away, trying not to pass out from exertion or boredom. Outside, the golf green was awash in that pretentious early morning light that always seems to mock people like me, night owls forced into daylight by obligation or guilt.

That's when I saw her. A white-haired woman walking briskly along the path in tennis whites and a ridiculously large sun visor, her limbs tanned, toned, and utterly defiant of age. There was something about her, perhaps the stubborn set of her jaw or determined angle of her stride, that reminded me — sharply and with unexpected force — of my paternal grandmother, my Mem! That unassuming saint. A woman of no great education or particular renown, who lived her life with quiet dignity and more strength than most cabinet ministers.

**

Mem was a devout Christian, thought never the sanctimonious type. Church on Sundays, casserole in hand for the grieving, and an almost suspiciously perfect cherry pie on birthdays and holidays. She bowled. She played softball. And she took care of my grandfather, who had one leg and the temperament of a 1950s hockey coach. For this, she neither complained nor demanded recognition. Like so many women of her era, she bore the weight of her family with the same silent grace that now seems to have been bred out of us.

In her mid-seventies, after decades of ten-pin bowling, we suggested, somewhat condescendingly, that she try five pin as it was supposedly easier, gentler, less likely to lead to a broken hip. She agreed, of course. She agreed to most everything, so long as it didn't contradict her sense of decency. And wouldn't you know it, she went on to win rookie-of-the-year at seventy-seven. I don't think I've been prouder of anyone in my life.

That moment — so humbling, so absurdly inspiring — has stayed with me. Whenever I've been asked to take on a new, particularly unfamiliar or daunting role (something that would make me want to run in the opposite direction, whether a promotion I didn't feel ready for, or some half-baked transformation initiative concocted by a roomful of consultants who use the word *learnings* like it's a real word), I would think of her. Of how she tried. Of how she didn't flinch. How she bowled with gusto and a smile on her face, and a score that would humble men half her age. And, in my own fumbling way, I have tried to lead. Not with the puffed-up swagger of corporate prophets or the gleaming ebullience of LinkedIn influencers, but with my Mem's quiet, stubborn kind of leadership — the kind that shows up, does the work, and doesn't need to post about it afterwards.

***

As I headed to the locker room looking forward to a relaxing post-workout steam and shower, I was reminded of a time, during one of my stints as a CEO, when I'd been struggling mightily with finding a way to overcome a significant shortfall due to declining revenues coupled with increasing expenses heading into the final quarter of the year. Not one to panic, but also under tremendous pressure, I brought in a few trusted members of my leadership team. One of the VPs, Carole, offered up advice about remaining calm, maintaining clarity of purpose and relying on the team. She recounted an example of leadership in action that resonated powerfully:

> Recently, while on a safari in one of Kenya's national parks, just before dusk, I witnessed something unforgettable: a lion hunt. As we prepared to exit the park — tourists are required to exit before sunset — our guide, who had been silently scanning the savannah, suddenly pulled over. He lifted his binoculars and focused intently on something far out in the grassland.
>
> There, in the golden haze of evening, we spotted them — a pride of lionesses. I counted seven. At the back, a male lion lingered, distant and observant. What followed was unmistakable: natural, disciplined, instinctive choreography.
>
> The lead lioness rose from the grassland. Ears flattened, she advanced in calculated, stealthy steps — ten metres at a time — then disappeared into the brush. Behind her, in perfect formation, the others followed in pairs, mirroring her every move. They needed no command; each instinctively knew her role, her path, her moment. In the rear, the male lion ambled forward, not as part of the hunt, but present nonetheless, as a quiet force anchoring the pride.
>
> Then suddenly the energy shifted. The lead lioness spotted a herd of water buffalo and

became fully alert. With a silent signal, she surged ahead. Her team responded instantly — fanning out, flanking from the left and right. The hunt had begun.

They gave everything they had. The lead lioness leapt onto the back of one buffalo. Her companions circled, biting at its heels, coordinating with the precision of a seasoned unit. The struggle continued fiercely for nearly twenty minutes. And then the buffalo escaped. The hunt was not successful.

But what struck me most happened after.

The lionesses regrouped. The lead lioness brushed gently against each of her companions, as if to say, "Well done. We were close. Next time, we will succeed." There was no blame, no retreat into ego. Only unity and mutual respect, the quiet dignity of a team that knew how to rise together even in the face of failure.

That moment has stayed with me.

As leaders — whether in the workplace, in our communities, or within our families — we often talk about vision, strategy and execution. But how often do we embody the deeper essence of what I saw in those lions? Leadership is not always being in front. It's about alignment. It's about instinct, trust, and having a team that moves with shared purpose, even when the outcome is uncertain.

The lions didn't win the hunt that day. But they won something greater: cohesion, resilience, and the kind of team spirit that guarantees eventual success. That day, I was reminded that a leader is only as powerful as the unity he or she inspires, and the strength of a team lies not in a single roar, but in their stride together.

Photo by Ahmed Galal. Source: Unsplash.

Now, Mem could certainly be referred to as a lioness. But so could the other women in my life. Janet, to whom I've been married for forty-three years of the fifty we've known each other, has always been an example of dedication. An exemplary student who worked briefly before raising our children, she returned to work and gave her all before retiring, fully embodying the principle of client priority — a true professional and an inspiration.

My daughter, Jo — a headstrong kid who could be incredibly challenging in her determination to get her way — learned to channel her spiritedness and has grown into an accomplished young woman. Full of confidence without ego, she is self-reflective and a life-long learner who achieves and contributes much professionally, and I am proud to see her rewarded in the workplace. She has not lost her tendency to challenge authority but has learned that proprietous behaviour can go a long way in succeeding with difficult superiors. Through my observation of her experiences, I've learned that there remains much to be done to provide equal pay and opportunities for working women, who still often bear the brunt of the caregiver role in the family sphere.

Reflecting on personal heroes always brings me back to my first heroes, my parents, whose self-sacrifice and courage were exemplified in the way they always put my sister and me first, prioritizing our activities and interests — camps, sports, and music lessons — and always opting for family vacations over exotic trips for the two of them alone. Though not highly educated, their monumental work ethic was passed down to their children and grandchildren. My admiration for them only increases as the years go by, especially their way of making the family a priority.

One of our family traditions, attending Major League Baseball games, grew over decades, and those early games with my dad and Pep expanded to include my son, Logan. In fact, our passion evolved into a whole new enterprise — an annual baseball trip. This became a quest to visit every stadium in the MLB, all thirty of them, sometimes with the whole family!

Logan, a feisty young man who excelled in sports including hockey and golf, decided to become an umpire at quite a young age. This provided many challenges as he was diminutive in stature. But luckily he was outsized in fearlessness. Now, acting as umpire is a true leadership position, one of great responsibility. Though the other players were larger, often towering over him, he was never intimidated, but focused on the role at hand, in which function and skill are critical to the outcome and flow of the sport.

Though hardly the star of the game, the umpire must lead behind the scenes to ensure the rules are enforced. At times of greatest conflict, when emotions run high and the pressure is on, the umpire needs to remain composed, objective, and clearheaded. If he makes an error, he must immediately correct it, learn from it, and move on.

There is no doubt Logan grew immensely from this experience as a person (and eventually in size too). Now an accomplished young man in the roles in his career and as a husband and parent, Logan must likewise make courageous decisions and stand by them, even if difficult or unpopular. I am very proud of him and his sister.

KEY TAKEAWAYS

- **Inspiration Comes from Unexpected Places** Everyday heroes — like grandmothers or lionesses — teach us that strength lies in perseverance, not spectacle.
- **Adaptability Requires Courage** Embracing unfamiliar roles or challenges with determination, even amid self-doubt, fosters growth and credibility.
- **Leadership Is a Team Sport** Success isn't about one individual's brilliance but the coordination, trust, and alignment of a cohesive team.
- **Failure Can Strengthen Unity** Like the lionesses, effective teams respond to setbacks not with blame but with grace, mutual respect, and renewed commitment.
- **Trust the Team's Instincts** Great leaders cultivate environments where team members intuitively understand their roles and act with confidence and accountability.
- **Stay Grounded in Purpose** Whether in corporate crisis or personal growth, calm clarity and alignment with core values are key to navigating turbulence.

Chapter 9

The Road North: Courage and Accountability

Photo by Andre Tan. Source: Unsplash.

The past is never dead. It's not even past.

— William Faulkner, from his novel *Requiem for a Nun*

In late April, as the Florida temperatures and humidity rose toward sweltering, Janet and I began the process of packing up the Jeep and shuttering our unit for the summer. I knew I would miss the tropical ocean-kissed mornings, palms catching the breeze by the calming blue Atlantic. But I was restless to leave the coastal pace behind and jump back into the busy hum of board meetings and lunches, catching up with colleagues, family, and friends. And I looked forward to spending time with the grandchildren — no doubt they'd grown.

The morning I was leaving I lingered over my coffee on the patio with Janet.

"Did we pack both sets of clubs, Jan?"

"Yes, of course we did."

"Are you looking forward to your last few days with your girlfriends?"

"Absolutely."

"And you'll be sure to behave yourselves?"

"We'll try. You too!" She wagged her finger at me.

She walked me to the car and gave me a kiss and a tight squeeze. "Travel safe now. Drive carefully, hear?"

"I will. Smooth flight and see you at home in three days. I'll pick you up at the airport."

The sun bled — low and unwavering — over Delray Beach, its gold sprawling over the pavement and burning the glass of my rear-view mirror. I gathered my driving staples: audiobooks, phone charger, Gatorade, some mixed nuts, and a Red Bull, and set myself north on the I-95. The highway's voice was a ceaseless murmur, the road humming its own hypnotic language under the wide, open sky. Delray receded like a memory, mutable as the palmetto shadows that lengthened across the morning.

Passing Orlando, I made a mental note to help plan a trip to Disney World with the grandkids the following year.

Several hours of short stories and a pit stop or two later, I approached the state of Georgia. The border is only a line, but as the pines thickened, Spanish moss clinging to oaks whose branches strain under the weight of history, my journey was momentarily fractured — a tire warning, one blinking eye upon the dashboard. I pulled off the road towards a tiny service station near Valdosta, red dust rising. Taking the opportunity to top up the gas and my snack supply along with air for the low tire, I then resumed my trajectory north, but my energy was beginning to flag. Luckily, I knew just the place to pause for the night.

Evening settled quietly over Savannah, the light slipping through moss-draped branches of old oaks that arched above the streets. The city felt timeless, its squares and cobblestones whispering of its long history. I walked in the hush, sipping sweet tea, letting the slow rhythm of the place sink in. Here, time seemed to loop back on itself — every shadow holding a trace of the past, every face a reminder of it. Savannah offered me a rare kind of rest, made sweeter because I knew it wouldn't last.

Morning started with coffee — strong, bitter, and essential — as I followed the highway deeper into the American landscape. By midday, Charleston opened up around me in a swirl of market chatter, pastel buildings, and salty air. I ate fried green tomatoes while street musicians played nearby. Heading north past Charlotte, the flat marshes of the Carolina low country gave way to the rolling green foothills of the Piedmont, rising gently from the red clay earth.

As I veered northwest through Virginia, the terrain began to shift dramatically — mountains rising, roads twisting, and the sky seeming closer. Sunlight filtered through chestnut and oak, greying into evening. Passing through the East River Mountain Tunnel into West Virginia felt almost symbolic — a threshold into the older, more introspective spine of America, a contrast that echoed the wonder of those long-ago trips through the Detroit Tunnel with my dad and Pep.

Somewhere just past the Kanawha River, as I wound my way up the Appalachian spine towards Beckley, West Virginia, I thought about the long shadows this land remembers. These wooded hollows and winding ridges once offered refuge not only to loggers and miners, but to those escaping something far more brutal: the bonds of slavery. West Virginia, though born in the crucible of the Civil War, had long before been a corridor of quiet resistance, I'd learned over the years passing through this place. Local families — Black and white — risked everything to help fugitives fleeing the Deep South. I occasionally passed old cabins and overgrown trails, long abandoned, that seemed to whisper of courage and peril amid the stillness of the trees.

Perched in the rugged folds of the Appalachian Plateau, Beckley is modest but quiet, and the surrounding land carries a hum of something ancient. The nearby New River Gorge, with its endless ridges, rust-streaked cliffs, and misty mornings is a breathtaking, familiar sight. It is a place where generations have lived close to the land — miners, farmers, and the Indigenous peoples who came long before them. The ground here feels layered with struggle and endurance. I began to ruminate on the self-determination and bravery of leaders, and this brought to mind two times in my career where I had to make hard decisions that required courage and resilience.

New River Gorge Bridge, West Virginia. Source: Picryl / Library of Congress.

***

All leaders require a sense of self-confidence in their ability to make a difference. They must seize the initiative, trust their own judgement and not be afraid to assert their views, even when contrary to popular opinion. But confidence should not be confused with inflated ego, and the difference speaks to character and selflessness. Self-assuredness without hubris, which can take years of experience to acquire, enables real leadership to arise when outcomes are not apparent or certain. Resilience is a quality that enables confidence and freedom from the fear of making mistakes. Part of leading an effective team is having the courage to accept criticism and acknowledge errors, make difficult decisions for the greater good of the team, and take swift action. Sometimes this responsibility includes letting people go, whether they are long-time employees or recent hires.

Once, as a young sales manager, I hired the wrong person for the job. Two months later came a national sales meeting with clients and personnel in Arizona, where my own recent promotion and the hiring of the new employee would be announced. I found out afterwards that my brand-new hire had been goofing off the entire first half of the event, designed for time to interact with clients and to build further understanding of the science behind our lead product. I thought long and hard about my error in judgment and decided that letting him go was the only way forward. Trust is critical in a strong work relationship, and courageous decisions often need to be made in public. When a poor choice has been made, it must be corrected with urgency. Of course, that correction must be handled professionally and with respect to the person impacted, and that was how I handled it.

Later on in my career, following a merger, I was faced with pulling together a new team for our company, one with the right balance to bridge a new culture, by combining the very best of the two former companies while leaving behind limiting behaviours and practices from the past. I was faced with replacing a respected, popular, and skilled individual, with whom I had worked for years. Many disagreed with my decision, but I knew it was the right one, and it proved to be so over time. But in the moment I felt isolated and even temporarily abandoned by those who disagreed with me. It was a difficult and painful process, affecting my personal relationship with the individual and changing it forever. But making the right decision — doing the hard work — regardless of personal consequences, while not always easy, is best for everyone in the long run.

***

I pulled off the I-64 just as the late light settled into the folds of the Appalachian hills and checked into a quiet roadside motel. At dinner, I asked a local about the area's Indigenous past. She paused before answering. "This was Shawnee land," she said simply. "Tecumseh's people. Before all this." The words carried more weight than she intended, I thought with a start.

Tecumseh. The name is etched into my own baptismal certificate — Tecumseh, Ontario. I've always taken quiet pride in that, though I knew little of the man himself growing up. Only later did I come to understand him not just as a warrior, but as a unifier, a leader with the courage to imagine a confederacy of nations that would resist dispossession not through domination, but through solidarity. He stood for something larger than his time and died for it.

It strikes me now how often we think of legacy as something clean and commemorated — etched in buildings or diplomas. But Tecumseh's legacy isn't tidy. It's scattered across unmarked trails, buried under highways, carried in whispers, and resurrected in places like this. Beckley may not remember him with plaques, but the earth does.

"After the Shawnee Wars and increasing pressure from settlers, most Native tribes were gradually forced westward. But Kanawha Valley, just north of here, contains burial mounds and artifacts that bear witness," my new friend continued, sharing with me her own Cherokee heritage on her father's side.

As I prepared to receive an honorary doctorate back home, I found myself thinking not of accolades, but of responsibilities — what must be built, rebuilt, or made right. Economic reconciliation is not charity. It's not optics. It is the continuation of the work leaders like Tecumseh began — an unfinished covenant with the land and the people who first called it home.

In the quiet of my motel room, I looked out at the ridgeline and thought of how leadership isn't about arrival, but about journeying, a pilgrimage. We don't lead from where we're going. We lead from where we've been — if we have the courage to remember.

As I set out the following morning, again, the flashing gauge indicated low pressure in the same rear tire. *Damn.* I kept one eye on the lookout for a rest stop, while anticipating a tranquil morning drive through Pennsylvania's scenic Laurel Highlands. But it would have to wait. A sudden jolt indicated a fissure, on a lonely stretch of highway, miles from the nearest service station. I began to feel a rising sense of panic.

Pulling over, it took me ages to find a roadside assistance provider, but when I finally did I was relieved that they could send someone within the hour. There was only one problem — the available technician did not speak a word of English. And I don't speak Spanish.

"We'll manage," I assured the dispatcher. I prayed that the one person I know fluent in that language would pick up the phone. I found the number on speed dial and waited for the serviceperson to arrive.

Tecumseh. Source: Shutterstock

Three years my junior, my sister, Viv, and I were close growing up, isolated as we were from the rest of the larger family network in Tecumseh and Windsor. We would dutifully visit the clan on end-of-summer road trips with our parents in between jaunts to Wasaga Beach, Parry Sound, and, best of all, Sauble Beach on Lake Huron. But as we grew, we grew further apart. While I visited my grandparents in Tecumseh, she would stay at home with our folks. And as we matured and I became laser focused on my career, travelling abroad constantly, she raised her family as a single mother and took up the slack as our parents got older and needed care. We didn't see each other often, as we lived very different lives.

Luckily for me, she had picked up Spanish years ago while dating a man from Peru, becoming quite proficient in a short time. I sighed with relief when, forty-five minutes later, an SUV arrived, and a young man emerged.

"Hey, sis," I said when she answered. "Two things, if you have a minute."

"Well hello, stranger. What's up?"

"Firstly, I wanted to make sure you got my email about the convocation and my honorary doctorate in June."

"Yes indeed. I'll be there. And?"

"I need your assistance as a translator." I told her about the tire, thanked her profusely, and gratefully handed the phone to my rescuer, interrupting his river of Spanish in which I could barely have hoped to tread water.

Viv, too, I realized, has always been my hero. Life was sometimes not easy or fair to her, yet every day she stepped out with quiet determination, intent on making the world a better place. Somehow, everyone she meets walks away feeling exactly that: the world *is* a great place, full of great people — people like her. She's raised two incredible children and played an instrumental role in the lives of her three grandchildren. She truly is amazing.

I resumed driving, the engine's thrum newly tentative, roads unwinding not only north but inward as I revisited early memories of Pep, Mem, and the Hardware — legacy of my great-grandfather, Jacques — and how selling it would be the end of an era. But I knew that I had built my own legacy, fashioning lessons gleaned over a lifetime into tools I'd honed, tools for leading and for living, that I would pass on to my children and future generations.

Crossing into Pennsylvania the journey climbed again. Passing through the picturesque fields and rolling hills of the Laurel Highlands, I recalled Pep's words about the

Underground Railroad and continued to trace its trajectory north. Nearby towns like Chambersburg and Harrisburg were hotbeds of abolitionist activity, I'd come to learn, with safe houses still standing along the route, some marked, some kept anonymous even now out of respect for their sacred secrecy.

And then there was Buffalo, that final underground portal, Canada just across the Niagara River — the Promised Land. It's hard to imagine the terror and triumph of that last stretch, especially in winter, when ice floes choked the current and patrols scoured the shoreline. But they came — men, women and children, carrying nothing but faith and each other. And people along the way chose to risk their safety for the sake of liberty.

I rolled down my window, letting the breeze carry the scent of wet leaves and mountain laurel. My journey north was easy — paved, mapped, and full of rest stops, albeit with one blown tire. But theirs? It was a journey carved in footsteps and silence. And in honouring that path, I was reminded of a deeper responsibility — to keep moving towards justice and coexistence, no matter how long the road.

KEY TAKEAWAYS

- **Legacy Shapes Leadership** Effective leaders must acknowledge and learn from the past — personal, cultural, and historical — to lead with depth and purpose.
- **Resilience Builds Integrity** Hard decisions — especially those that impact others — demand courage and emotional endurance. True leadership shows up when outcomes are uncertain.
- **Responsibility over Recognition** Honours and titles matter less than the duty to advance justice, reconciliation, and collective progress.
- **Courage to Stand Alone** Leaders sometimes walk lonely paths, especially when making unpopular but necessary decisions for the greater good.
- **Pilgrimage, Not Arrival** Leadership is a continual journey, not a destination. It requires reflection, movement, and recommitment to values along the way.
- **Justice Requires Action** Remembering the struggles of others — enslaved peoples, Indigenous nations, or marginalized workers — is not enough. Leadership demands ongoing action toward equity and reconciliation.

Chapter 10

Generosity and Humility:

Good to Great Leadership

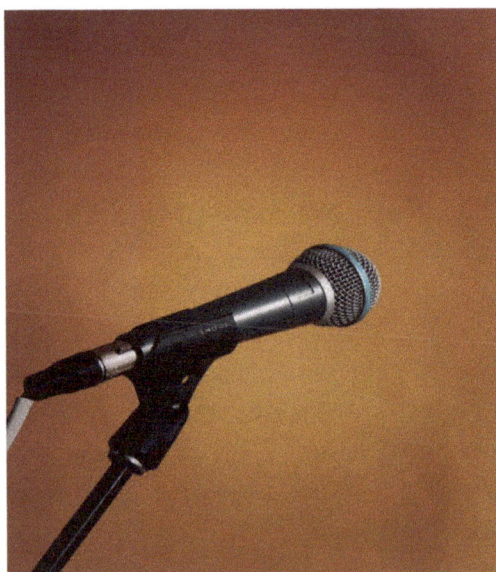

Photo by Jon Tyson. Source: Unsplash.

After an unseasonably rainy May and first week of June in Toronto and a sufficient healing period for the old knee, the sun finally came out and it was time to hit the links. I threw my gear into the trunk and headed out to Woodbridge for an early morning tee-off. Switching channels on satellite radio, all the American stations were abuzz about the same topic — unrest in California: riots protesting ICE and mass deportations; the calling in of the National Guard, the Navy, and God knows what else.

What would Pep think about all this, I wondered. It would be as foreign to him as a spaceship from Mars landing in the middle of the cornfield during one of our forays to the granary to pick up thirty bags of feed for the Hardware. Those days were so different from today; the town — even our new neighbourhood in the city to some extent — had a true sense of community. People were intimately involved in each other's lives, like one big family. Personal relationships were everything, were our foundation. Pep knew everyone in town, and everyone knew and respected him in turn. People today in big cities may be more sophisticated, more tech savvy. But they are also more isolated, their relationships impersonal. We have become online consumers, social media surfers from our own little domains; that old-fashioned small-town camaraderie has all but disappeared.

Pep's leadership qualities were all about conversations with neighbours, asking about the kids, grandkids, parents, cousins. *Caring* about them. Helping each customer to find just the right tool, the right component, part, whatever they needed; to find simple solutions to the daily tasks of living. On the other hand, Pep was quite a character; he was a very social person who loved to entertain, enjoyed his drink and a good party, and knew how to have fun and share a good time. And it rubbed off on me!

***

A few years ago, I found myself working in London, England, which sounds more glamorous than it was, unless you consider windowless conference rooms, too many lanyards, and tepid coffee glamorous. But one particular evening we managed to shake loose from the corporate routine and drift into the realm of "Did that really happen?"

It was a warm, particularly lovely London night, and a group of us — ten tired, slightly overcooked professionals — decided to have dinner and drinks. The meetings were done, the decks had been presented, the stakeholders thoroughly aligned. We had earned our pints. And, apparently, our rickshaws.

Yes, rickshaws. Don't ask why. It seemed fun at the time. Somewhere between Piccadilly and Mayfair, our drivers decided to turn the trip into a race, pedalling through the city with the kind of reckless abandon usually reserved for Bond chases or lost tourists. I'm pretty sure we were violating at least three minor traffic laws and possibly the Geneva Convention.

We pulled up to our hotel a little after ten, laughing, windblown, dressed in the international uniform of casual — jeans, leather jackets, and the unmistakable air of having just discovered the cocktail bar still open. That's when my friend John noticed a group of tuxedoed gentlemen having a cigarette outside the side door. He recognized one of them and approached the formally dressed group. In a display of British charm mixed with perhaps a bit too much champagne, John's colleague greeted him enthusiastically and after a bit of chitchat, invited us to crash what turned out to be the formal awards banquet for a very large, very important consulting firm.

Naturally, we said "Yes, why not?" We followed John's new-found friend into the ballroom in our casual wear without a second thought and were escorted to a far corner in the back of the room — strategically hidden near the bar, conveniently close to the band. With the reckless optimism of characters in a musical, or Ferris Bueller skipping school, I decided this was the moment to order some champagne. Then I had an idea.

I sauntered over to the AV desk — of course, they had one — chatted up the technician and asked if I could borrow the microphone when the band finished. This had been "cleared," I assured him with the gentleman who had invited us in, to whom I now pointed; the technician acknowledged him and then looked back at me. I smiled like someone absolutely, one hundred percent not authorized to do what I was about to do. He gave me the mic.

The band played the final number, the lights dimmed, and suddenly I was up on the stage standing in front of a few hundred impeccably dressed consultants and their spouses, holding a glass of champagne, and wearing my leather jacket, clearly out of place.

"Good evening," I began. "I'm with the firm." (Which, technically, wasn't entirely untrue. I *did* work in consulting and I *was* invited to join them. That night, during their dinner.)

I congratulated the award winners, pointed to the glowing slogans on the screens around the room — things like "People First" and "Innovate to Elevate" — and I captured short quips regarding each and every one of them. In doing so, I gave the kind of rousing speech that would have made Cameron Frye proud.

"Also," I added casually, "my team in the corner there — yes, the ones dressed like they just walked out of a Bon Jovi video — are top performers, too. We are the winners of the firm's awards in the US!" The spotlight found them, obligingly, as they roared with laughter, clapping and waving. And for one brief and glorious moment, we were the heroes of someone else's corporate event. I thanked the crowd for their time and patience and calmly left the stage. Returning to my friends at the back of the room, we were absolutely buckled with laughter.

Eventually, the dinner ended, as all good things do, and we took what remained of our champagne into Hyde Park and toasted to … well … everything. The absurdity. The sheer luck. The fact that no one had called security. Then, as if we hadn't had enough fun and the night not yet over, a few of us found a pub still open and shared one last round, like aging rock stars on the tail end of a reunion tour.

The next morning, I woke up at eleven. My phone had twelve messages, all from John. The last one said "Bueller, Bueller, Bueller. That was a wonderful evening, Ferris. Have a great day." From that day on, I was no longer Brad. I was Ferris. And honestly, I didn't mind.

Having fun is part of leading from the front, just enjoying your time with colleagues and those who have become friends; being front and centre to create a delightful atmosphere; letting go of ego, of agenda. Playing together, enjoying time together. Being a team in leisure as well as work.

∗∗∗

As the radio announcer droned on about blocked streets, tear gas, and arrests, I couldn't help but worry about failed leadership built on ego, on force. Polarization and partisanship were allowing extremism and baseless hatred to threaten liberal democracy, unravel the very fabric of society. Where was the humility in leadership? Ego has replaced self-confidence, while principles of morality and simple human values are getting lost in the confusion. Disruption has led to destruction, violence. There is a lack of communication, a lack of referent power — the ability to influence by example, trust, and loyalty, rather than by hubris, self-righteousness, and whim.

Canada, too, is not immune to the emergence of selfishness and poor leadership. Leaders have promised to improve internal and international trade relationships, develop our natural resources while having made commitments to consulting with First Nations in these decisions, to act as partners. But obligations, for example to ensure equal access to proper drinking water, have failed after decades of inaction. Our leaders can and must do better to effectively collaborate with Indigenous and other minorities.

I turned off the radio as I arrived at the club gate and was waved in by security, towards grounds groomed to perfection — a green carpet as far as the eye could see, rolling hills and acres of dense forest beyond, belying the location close to the city. I pulled into the parking lot beside the elegantly rustic clubhouse, feeling gratitude for the opportunity to enjoy this beautiful place and join my buddies for a friendly game of golf. I paused for a moment, smiling as I recalled a simple lesson about the power of humility from an anecdote related by my friend Adrian during our last round of golf:

> Shortly after relocating to Europe to assume a new role as vice president, I made a decision that, at the time, felt routine.
>
> I had registered for a professional training seminar in Portugal; I booked my flight, reserved a hotel, and confirmed my attendance. As an executive, I had always exercised autonomy in selecting development opportunities, especially when they aligned with my role and fell within my

budget. However, upon returning, I was summoned to the CEO's office.

He informed me very directly, that he had become aware of my trip and that any similar travel had to be pre-approved by him. I was stunned. This wasn't how things had worked in the past thirty-seven years of my career. In every leadership role I had held, professional development was not only encouraged, it was expected.

In that moment, I had two options.

I could have pushed back. I could have defended my actions, emphasized the norms of executive discretion, and pointed out that my intentions were aligned with the company's goals. And a younger version of me might have done just that.

But this was a new country, a new culture, and a new CEO. I understood instinctively that what might feel like assertiveness to me could be interpreted as defiance to him. So I took a different path.

I calmly told him I hadn't been aware that such travel required his pre-approval, and I assured him that moving forward, I would ensure he was informed in advance. As soon as I said those words, I saw his posture shift. He relaxed. He smiled. He told me he appreciated my understanding, that this was the normal process, and that he was glad we were aligned.

From that day forward, we developed an excellent working relationship, one built on trust and mutual respect. I can't say that moment in his office was the single turning point, but I do believe it helped lay the foundation, and I have never once regretted choosing humility over ego.

There's strength in knowing when to stand firm — and a deeper strength in knowing when to step back. Leadership isn't always about asserting authority. Sometimes, it's about listening, adapting, and choosing the path that serves the bigger picture.

That day reminded me that respect is not lost in an apology — especially when it's given with intention and integrity.

KEY TAKEAWAYS

- **Be Human and Approachable** Laughter and lightness build strong, loyal teams.
- **Adapt to Culture and Context** Effective leadership requires sensitivity to new environments — what works in one organization or culture may not in another.
- **Lead with Emotional Intelligence** Recognize how your actions may be perceived by others; assertiveness in one context can be seen as defiance in another.
- **Choose Humility Over Ego** True strength lies in knowing when to stand down to preserve relationships and build trust.
- **Respect and Flexibility Strengthen Leadership** Leadership isn't about always being right — it's about serving the bigger picture and acting with grace.

Chapter 11

The Hardware: Spring Convocation

Photo by Eugen Str. Source: Unsplash.

The sun shone brilliantly in a clear blue sky over King's College Circle as our procession, clad in variously coloured robes, entered stately Convocation Hall , to the solemn strains of Bach emanating from the building's organ. Hundreds of eager graduates, young faces beaming, were seated on the main floor, their guests ensconced in respective tiered balconies under the beautiful, blue, vaulted dome edged in white mouldings. As we found our seats on the dais,

I looked up and waved to my family and a few friends on a loge to the right; I looked forward to celebrating with them after the ceremony at the small reception Janet had arranged at a nearby restaurant.

The university chancellor, Les Small, a local business leader, entrepreneur, and celebrity investor on a television show, tall and striking in his black and yellow robe, delivered the land acknowledgement, after which he and President Merkler had an exchange in Latin, explaining the proceedings. Then the president provided an official welcome and brief remarks, saluted the graduating class of the Abelson School of Management, and announced that I would be honoured that day adding a brief description of my career and connection to the university. And then he called up the person who would introduce me. It was none other than my old friend Senator Carrie Fley, who smiled warmly at me as she approached the microphone before delivering the following remarks:

> I have worked with many accomplished leaders over my career. But every now and then, if you are fortunate enough, you encounter someone who doesn't just lead well — they teach you what leadership truly is. For me, that was Brad Stuart.
> Brad wasn't just the President and CEO of PharmaLabs — a commanding post in one of the most vital industries of our time — he was a steward of values I've come to associate with great statesmanship: humility, presence, integrity, and shared purpose.
> When I first met him, I was pitching a campaign for the University of Toronto. He could have towered over the moment with corporate polish and ego; instead, he began simply: "Call me

Brad." It's no small thing when people at the top insist on meeting you eye to eye. That subtle act of equality paved the way for an honest, rigorous, and meaningful conversation.

He asked tough questions. He listened. He expected intelligence. But most importantly, he projected what Madeleine Albright championed throughout her life: the belief that consensus, preparedness, and shared ownership build movements, not just moments. His "yes" to that campaign wasn't transactional — it was transformational. Together, we helped shape the Gertrude McPhee Academic Learning Centre, not because one person powered it into reality, but because a group — under wise guidance — believed enough to commit to it.

Years later, when I became a CEO for the first time, I leaned on Brad as a mentor. I was afraid — unsure, unseasoned, trying to live up to the idea of perfection that so many women in leadership are unfairly expected to embody.

I called him in total vulnerability. "Brad, I don't know what I'm doing."

He didn't try to fix everything. Instead, he responded with truth, humour, and clarity: "Welcome to being a CEO."

I protested — I had to look strong, unflappable, commanding. And he said something I've never forgotten:

"Why would you have all the answers? That's why you have a team. Don't be afraid to say you don't know. That's what builds trust."

He wasn't telling me to step back — he was teaching me a different form of strength: informed vulnerability. As Secretary Albright would remind us in the midst of foreign diplomacy: leadership is not about bluster or certainty. It's about making space for others to rise alongside you — and having the moral courage to admit what you don't know and then work tirelessly to learn it.

And, yes, he reminded me: bathrooms are for meltdowns. Gather yourself — then return with dignity and resolve. Even great leaders need moments of release, especially when the stakes are high.

Throughout my journey at Youth Line SOS, I have returned to Brad's advice often. He reminded me that the loneliest place is not the top but the top without allies. And that every member of your organization, from reception to C-suite, deserves to be seen as a contributor, a leader, and a human being.

In difficult moments — like growing two hundred and fifty percent during the pandemic, when the world had shut down and youth mental health was in crisis — it wasn't my strength alone that led. It was our collective will to show up for each other and for the youth we serve. We could not fail — because failure wasn't just business, it was life or death.

Brad's words echoed in those moments. "You are all in it together. But the buck does stop with you."

Leadership is responsibility, as Albright would say. Not a platform, but a promise. I made space for my team, led from honesty, and forged ahead fortified by the courage to admit what I didn't know — and the conviction to find out.

Madeleine Albright once said, "There is a special place in hell for women who don't help each other." Brad Stuart may not be a woman — but he fully embodies that ethos of helping others rise. His voice has been with me in every challenge, policy decision, budget negotiation, and crisis response. His advice wasn't just support — it was principled guidance drawn from a deep understanding of what it means to lead with conscience.

And that's what I've passed on. To my team. To the next generation of CEOs. To everyone listening. I share his wisdom, like an ambassador carries the voice of a nation. Whenever someone on my team hears "This is a Brad Stuart moment," they know exactly what that means: truth, integrity, support, and the courage to face uncertainty head on.

From the youth of Canada and from me — your student in leadership and humanity — thank you, Brad.

I was almost dumbstruck by her kind remarks and immeasurably grateful for them, and I said as much after accepting the award, thanking her profusely. And after I gave thanks to the University of Toronto for bestowing upon me this honour, I then delivered my own prepared remarks:

Good afternoon graduates, families, faculty, and honoured guests.

Imagine yourself standing in the middle of a well-stocked hardware store. Not just any store — but *your* store. It's stocked with every tool you'll need to build the career, the team, and the life you dream of. Today, we talk about how to use those tools — not just to succeed — but to strive for excellence in everything you do and reach your fullest potential.

First, the hammer.

It's direct, it gets things done. It's the symbol of productivity, competence, and strength. Over the course of your education, you've mastered the basics: skills, discipline, and determination. Now you will take initiative, find your own path and deliver results.

You will learn to shape your environment.

But remember this: a hammer can build, or it can break. It's your values — your purpose — that decide which. And so you must always choose to build, by always acting with intention, not reaction.

Next, the tape measure.

It doesn't work alone — it's used in partnership, helping others find their place, align their goals, measure progress. Greatness is not a solo act; you will measure not just tasks, but their impact.

With your team, you will define success clearly, then collaborate to build it.

Effective people see the blueprint before they pick up the tool.

The tape measure reminds us: no one succeeds in isolation. Which brings us to networking — not the kind you do with a stack of business cards, but the kind you build with trust, generosity, and shared goals. But more on this later, after we've gathered all our primary tools. Now comes the power drill.

Efficient. Focused. Precise. It gets the job done faster, better, and smarter.

Organizing people and resources toward the effective pursuit of objectives by focusing on what matters, not just what is urgent, and prioritizing long-term effectiveness over short-term business.

A power drill used with purpose builds faster and better. Lead with clarity and focus.

But here's the thing: even the best drill can strip a screw if it's used with force instead of finesse. Competence without care becomes control. This is where humility begins to matter.

Then there's the level.

It doesn't make noise. It doesn't take credit. But it ensures everything is balanced and aligned. You inspire high performance standards and set a vision worth following.

The level doesn't force — it invites alignment. And great leaders know the best visions are shared. Your job isn't to be the smartest in the room. It's to build a room full of people who want to build something together.

By building a culture of mutual benefit, not competition, and leading with fairness and purpose, the level balances everything. Great leaders build trust by lifting everyone up.

And finally, the toolbox.

It holds the hammer, the tape measure, the drill, the level — and more. It's *not* the flashiest piece in the store. But it's the one that brings everything else together.

Great leaders are paradoxes: fiercely ambitious — for a cause greater than themselves — humble in person, but relentless in pursuit of excellence.

They listen deeply — even to those they don't agree with — and lead with humility. They don't build empires; they build legacies through collaboration and character.

And the most powerful feature of the toolbox? It shares its tools. It multiplies its impact through others.

The toolbox holds everything; great leaders don't just build — they elevate.

In today's world, no toolkit is complete without acknowledging one of the most powerful new instruments at our disposal: artificial intelligence.

AI is a remarkable tool. It can analyze vast datasets in seconds, automate repetitive tasks, generate content, optimize operations, and even simulate decision-making. It's like having a smart assistant that never sleeps — an advanced multi-tool in your leadership kit.

But here's the truth: AI is not the leader. You are.

AI can process information — but it can't care.

It can forecast trends — but it can't inspire trust.

It can generate answers — but it can't ask the right, human questions.

It can optimize systems — but it can't build culture.

It can simulate empathy — but it can't feel it.

AI can assist. It can enhance. It can even challenge us to be better thinkers. But it cannot replace the integrity, vision, and character of a human leader who listens, adapts, and connects with people.

So use AI wisely. Let it sharpen your insights, speed up your workflow, and unlock new levels of efficiency. But never delegate your values. Never outsource your courage. Never forget that leadership — real leadership — is not about having the most tools. It's about knowing *when* to use them, *why* they matter, and *who* you're building for.

The best leaders don't fear AI. They lead it — with wisdom, empathy, and purpose.

But where do all these tools hang when in use for a project? On the pegboard wall, a metaphor for your network, your community of people with gifts, knowledge, and ideas.

In a hardware store, a tool left in a drawer gets rusty. On the wall, it's visible, accessible, shared. Your network is your pegboard — it holds the mentors, colleagues, peers, and partners who keep you sharp, challenged, and supported.

You don't compete with them, you build with them by nurturing meaningful connections and shared growth.

Don't collect people like trophies. Forge connections by building real mutual relationships. Be the one who checks in, who offers help before it's asked for, who shows up without needing a reason.

Synergy turns tools into teams.

But perhaps the most important thing for you to remember on your journey is that your tools need care, and so do you. As Stephen Covey says, you must sharpen the saw.

Invest in your physical, mental, emotional, and spiritual well-being.

Learn continuously, including Canadian and world history. Rest deliberately. Reflect regularly.

A dull tool weakens the builder. Keep yourself sharp.

In conclusion, here's your blueprint, Class of 2025:

Today, you graduate not just with knowledge, but with a toolkit of principles, habits, and purpose.

Go and build.

Build businesses that serve.

Build teams that thrive.

Build networks that empower.

Build a life aligned with your values.

The tools don't make the leader — you do. From habit to hammer, from vision to values — go build something great.

Final Reflections

A Life in Service and

Leadership

It has been said that one's career resembles a great campaign — full of unexpected turns, uphill battles, and moments of triumph hard-won through perseverance. Mine has been no different. There have been the dizzying highs and the daunting lows, the anxious moments before the charge, and the quiet satisfaction of work well done. Yet, it is not the ease of the journey that defines us, but the courage with which we meet its many trials.

As I walked upon the stage to receive the honorary degree, I was struck not by the pomp of the moment, but by the quiet truth that experience — above all — is the greatest teacher. With the benefit of hindsight, one may smile at former missteps or savour past victories. But it is in the very midst of challenge, in the fog and fire of real time, that we are forged into who we are meant to become.

Throughout my life, I have had the privilege to stand in the company of great leaders — not always adorned in rank or renown, but leaders nonetheless. From my earliest days in a humble hardware store, I witnessed the nobility of everyday leadership. My grandparents, parents, aunts, and uncles —

they were the first to show me what it meant to lead: not by edict, but by example; not by show, but by steadfast service. And over the years, my wife and children have taught me these lessons many times over.

The foundations of any enduring leadership are not built in marble halls, but in the quiet, unglamorous moments where one chooses decency over expedience, courage over comfort, and the welfare of others over personal gain. This, I believe, is the truest form of leadership, and the finest education one can ever receive.

In the many years that followed, I have encountered that same spirit in others time and again. It has been a privilege beyond words. And I say this not with sentimentality, but with firm conviction: I have been blessed.

Let every person find their own "hardware" — their starting point, however modest. For in that place of origin lies the compass for a lifetime of meaningful service. May you hold fast to it, especially in the storm.

And remember leadership, in its purest form, is not the pursuit of glory, but the quiet, enduring will to serve others, come what may.

Bradley Stuart

Bookshelf

Leadership and Organizational Health

Ken Blanchard and **Spencer Johnson**. *The One Minute Manager*. William Morrow, 1982.

A simple framework for effective leadership through clear goals, praise, and constructive feedback.

Jim Collins. *Good to Great: Why Some Companies Make the Leap ... and Others Don't*. Harper Business, 2001.

A research-driven look at what separates great companies from good ones, emphasizing disciplined leadership and culture.

Patrick Lencioni. *The Advantage: Why Organizational Health Trumps Everything Else in Business*. Jossey-Bass, 2012.

Argues that healthy organizational culture is the most powerful driver of long-term success.

Patrick Lencioni. *The Four Obsessions of an Extraordinary Executive: A Leadership Fable*. Jossey-Bass, 2000.

A concise fable that reveals four key principles leaders must embrace to build healthy organizations, with a focus on clarity, alignment, and communication.

Personal Growth and Habits

Marc Champagne. *Personal Socrates: Questions That Will Upgrade Your Life from Legends and World-Class Performers.* Baronfig, 2021.

Explores how asking better questions can lead to greater clarity, performance, and purpose.

Stephen R. Covey. *The 7 Habits of Highly Effective People: Powerful Lessons in Personal Change.* Free Press, 1989.

Timeless principles for personal and professional effectiveness, grounded in character and integrity.

Tim Ferriss. *Tools of Titans: The Tactics, Routines, and Habits of Billionaires, Icons, and World-Class Performers.* Houghton Mifflin Harcourt, 2016.

A collection of productivity tools and mental models from high achievers across industries.

Cal Newport. *Deep Work: Rules for Focused Success in a Distracted World.* Grand Central Publishing, 2016.

A practical guide to cultivating focused, distraction-free concentration in a world filled with noise. Newport argues that the ability to do "deep work" is becoming increasingly rare — and increasingly valuable — for those who want to thrive professionally and creatively.

Jay Shetty. *Think Like a Monk: Train Your Mind for Peace and Purpose Every Day.* Simon & Schuster, 2020.

A guide to applying ancient monastic wisdom to modern life, with practices to overcome negativity, develop discipline, and build a purpose-driven mindset.

Change and Adaptability

Spencer Johnson. *Who Moved My Cheese? An Amazing Way to Deal with Change in Your Work and in Your Life*. G.P. Putnam's Sons, 1998.

A simple parable that illustrates how people react to change and why adaptability matters.

John P. Kotter. *Leading Change.* Harvard Business Review Press, 1996.

A foundational guide to change management, Kotter outlines an eight-step process for leading successful organizational transformation, emphasizing urgency, vision, and stakeholder engagement.

Tanya Talaga. *All Our Relations: Finding the Path Forward.* CBC Massey Lectures. House of Anansi Press, 2018.

A powerful reflection on intergenerational trauma, Indigenous resilience, and the importance of community and healing.

Communication and Relationships

Dale Carnegie. *How to Win Friends and Influence People.* Simon and Schuster, 1936.

A classic guide to building trust, influencing others, and mastering human connection.

Patrick Lencioni. *The Five Dysfunctions of a Team: A Leadership Fable.* Jossey-Bass, 2002.

A business fable that reveals common barriers to team performance and how to overcome them.

Kim Scott. *Radical Candor: Be a Kick-Ass Boss Without Losing Your Humanity*. St. Martin's Press, 2017.

A practical guide to building strong professional relationships by caring personally while challenging directly. Scott introduces a framework for giving feedback, leading teams, and creating a culture of trust and accountability.

Creativity and Personal Mastery

Michael J. Gelb. *How to Think Like Leonardo da Vinci: Seven Steps to Genius Every Day*. Dell Publishing, 1998.

A dynamic guide to unlocking creativity and intellectual potential by exploring the habits and mindset of Leonardo da Vinci. Gelb outlines seven principles — from curiosity and independent thinking to refining the senses — that help readers develop their own genius.

Entrepreneurship and Resilience

Phil Knight. *Shoe Dog: A Memoir by the Creator of Nike*. Scribner, 2016.

A candid and compelling memoir by Nike's co-founder, tracing the brand's early struggles and risky decisions, offering a behind-the-scenes look at the grit, vision, and perseverance required to build a global company.

Global Affairs and Strategic Thinking

Madeleine Albright. *Memo to the President Elect: How We Can Restore America's Reputation and Leadership*. Harper, 2008.

A former Secretary of State outlines key global challenges and offers pragmatic advice to future US presidents on diplomacy, national security, and rebuilding international trust.

Technology and Innovation

Bill Gates. *Source Code: My Beginnings*. Penguin Random House, 2024.

A reflective memoir from Bill Gates tracing his early years, the formation of Microsoft, and the intellectual and ethical roots of his worldview and work.

Sally Percy. *Disruptors: How 15 Successful Businesses Defied the Norm*. Kogan Page, 2020.

A collection of profiles on bold entrepreneurs and executives who challenged conventional thinking to drive transformation in their industries. Percy explores what makes disruptors different and how their mindset fuels innovation and resilience.

Servant Leadership

James C. Hunter. *The Servant: A Simple Story About the True Essence of Leadership*. Crown Business, 1998.

A leadership fable that explores the power of servant leadership through the story of a businessman who attends a retreat and learns that true influence comes from humility, service, and character rather than authority or control.

Spirituality and Meaning

Rainn Wilson. *Soul Boom: Why We Need a Spiritual Revolution*. Hachette Go, 2023.

The actor and Bahá'í-inspired thinker explores modern spirituality, calling for a deeper collective soul-searching beyond materialism and tribalism.

Time, Productivity, and Philosophy

Oliver Burkeman. *Four Thousand Weeks: Time Management for Mortals*. Farrar, Straus and Giroux, 2021.

A thoughtful and philosophical look at time management, reminding readers that life is short and encouraging them to focus on meaning over busyness.

Acknowledgements

Photo by Jeremy Hynes. Source: Unsplash.

A Note of Thanks from Michael Cloutier

My family has been well represented in the preceding pages. Again, it all starts and ends with you, I am nothing without you and your love/support.

I could fill entire pages with the names of those who've played a critical role in my leadership journey. I know there's a real risk of unintentionally leaving someone out and, if I do, please know it's an oversight of memory **not** of appreciation. The people you'll read about here are outside of my family, but they are no less cherished. And yes — with permission — your names are absolutely *not* changed to protect anyone.

Randi Madonik Skurka: What an absolute joy and blessing you are. I'm *so* grateful you agreed to collaborate on this project and help bring it into the world. I can say without a shred of doubt that this book would never have been completed without you. I continue to be amazed at how often I meet new people who become dear friends almost instantly. Thank you for being you.

Tom Potter: The GOAT of leadership in my world and in the eyes of so many others. No one is wiser, kinder, or more committed to ensuring the success of those around them. You've been quoted by countless people, admired by even more, and you've always had my back. I am truly blessed to call you a friend and colleague.

Richard Hinson: From you, I learned the meaning of courage, especially when facing unpopular decisions. I admire your unwavering sense of justice, and your decision to return the company to the local leadership team was both admirable and inspiring. It created opportunities for so many people to shine.

Jim "Red" Payne: After my grandfather, you are the greatest relationship builder I've ever met. I've always been struck by how people light up when they see you and by the genuine warmth you bring to every interaction.

John Dickey: You took a green-as-grass, irreverent man-child and taught him focus and discipline. Your sense of humour was underappreciated by too many but treasured by those who understood it.

Anne Tomalin: Quiet leadership. Brilliance and confidence without a shred of ego. The most powerful leader in times of chaos and blessed with a wicked sense of humour.

Kathy Hay: While you might say I've helped you most, I'm letting the world know the opposite is true. You've modelled courage, determination, selflessness, and an unwavering commitment to society in every role you've taken on. Our conversations and my observations of your leadership in action have been deeply inspiring.

To the many others who contributed stories, memories, and wisdom — including Amita Kent, Jim Hall, and John Savoie — thank you for your generosity, your insights, and — above all — your friendship.

Company Crew — To my peers, colleagues, and friends. You know who you are!

Anita, Anna, Ann, Angelique, Angie, Brad, Bob, Bill, Carrie, Caryn, Carol, Claire-Marie, Dennis, Denis, Dan, Grant, Gerry, Gil, Harold, James, Janice, Jennifer, Jordan, Jerry, Joe, Karen, Linda, Lynda, Mac, Mary, Mo, Matt, Nancy, Paul, Peter, Phil, Philip, Philippe, Patricia, Pam, Pamela, Ryan, Richard, Rick, Ron, Sam, Steve, Stephany, Tim, Terry, Teresa, Theresa, Toni, Tony, Vicky, William, Xavier, Zunobia.

A Note of Thanks from Randi Madonik Skurka

First and foremost, I would like to thank Mike Cloutier for giving me this wonderful opportunity and for sharing with me his insight, wisdom, book list, favourite television series, music, and adventures. It has been an absolute pleasure to work with you, and I am honoured to call you my friend.

To Tom Robson, who introduced me to Mike after we connected on LinkedIn, I can't thank you enough for your thoughtfulness, kindness, and insight in proposing this productive collaboration.

To my friend and Toronto Writers' Centre colleague Victoria — thank you for your kind support, expertise, encouragement and delicious baking over the years.

To my friend and mentor Joe Kertes — thank you for your invaluable, kind, and patient support, encouragement, example, and words of wisdom all along my writing journey.

To my siblings, Robyn and Allan — thank you for your lifelong support, love, and interest in all my endeavours.

To my dad Sam and late mom Dodie — thank you for providing me with so much — life, love, values, education, and for your inspiring perseverance in the face of life's challenges.

To my children and grandchildren — thank you for being my beacon of light.

About the Authors

Michael Cloutier is an accomplished Canadian business leader and advisor with over forty years in the Life Sciences sector. He is well respected for his leadership skills, business acumen, coaching and mentoring accomplishments, and is an experienced business school lecturer who spearheaded fundraising for the construction of the Sheridan College Hazel McCallion Campus Student Centre.

Over the past twenty-five years, Mike was General Manager, President and CEO of five major pharmaceutical firms and one nonprofit organization, the Canadian Diabetes Association (now Diabetes Canada). In 2017, Mike founded a global consulting practice, Accelera Canada Ltd., which was acquired by Eversana Life Sciences Services in 2021. Over the past four years Mike has evolved a more entrepreneurial profile and engaged in the start-up of a number of Life Sciences related companies, most recently, strategic HR firm Bridgebright, www.bridgebright.com.

Randi Madonik Skurka is a Canadian writer of fiction and nonfiction. After working as a community pharmacist for three decades, she completed an MA in Jewish Studies and began to write about her family history while enrolled at the Humber School for Writers. Her opinion pieces have appeared in national and international media, and she has recently completed a historical novel based on the saga of resistance and survival of two sisters during World War II. Her website can be found at www.randiskurka.com.